TEMPLE TALKS...

about Autism and Sensory Issues

The World's Leading Expert on Autism Shares Her Advice and Experiences

DR. TEMPLE GRANDIN

Author of *Thinking in Pictures*

Temple Talks ... about Autism and Sensory Issues

All marketing and publishing rights guaranteed to and reserved by:

Sensory World

A proud imprint of Sensory Focus, LLC

Phone and Fax: 888•507•2193

Online: www.sensoryworld.com

Email: info@sensoryworld.com

ISBN: 9781935567424

Contents

Contents

Introduction

Let me start out by telling you a little about myself.

hen I was two-and-a-half years old, I could not talk. I had the classic symptoms of autism. I have a typical family history. On my father's side, there are four generations of bankers. On my mother's side, there's an engineer trained at the Massachusetts Institute of Technology, who co-invented the autopilot used in airplanes. We have a history of anxiety and depression on both sides of the family. The folks on my mother's side are intellectually gifted and good at visual thinking. There are food allergies on my father's side, and some traits of Asperger's syndrome on both sides of the family. These are continuous traits that are not simply the result of Mendelian inheritance; the genetics are extremely complicated.

Fortunately, I was very lucky to get into a good early education intervention program at the age of two-and-a-half years. I went to a small speech therapy school two teachers ran from the basement of their house. They did a lot of interventions that were similar to what we know today as applied behavior analysis (ABA). By the time I was four, I was talking. My speech teacher actually invented ABA, but she didn't know it. When I was three years old, my mother hired a nanny, who played constant turn-taking games with my sister and me. It is so important to teach these kids how to take turns. That and other simple "manners" are essential to their development. I will talk more about that later.

A good teacher should be gently insistent and must instinctively know how much to push these kids. You can push some kids really hard right away. But you need to be a lot more gentle with others to keep them from going into sensory overload. A recent study at UCLA with functional MRI indicated that the brain of an individual with autism overreacts to sensory stimulation. The overreaction occurs in both the sensory cortex and emotional centers that activate fear.

So how can you figure out which kind of kid you're dealing with? Well, if every trip to a large supermarket results in a giant screaming fit, then there are probably some severe sensory issues. These kids might need a quiet environment free of distracting background noise and bright visual stimuli. Some of these children may have problems hearing and seeing at the same time, so please be aware of that.

Teachers, and the way they teach, are so important to these kids in early life. We need to get plenty of hours of one-on-one teaching. It is important to keep pushing kids with autism and sensory issues to learn new skills. Although, be aware that if you push too hard, they will not progress. And remember: no sudden surprises, or you will risk the child shutting down or having a meltdown.

One problem today is that too many kids with autism do shut down and they shut down so much they risk becoming recluses. A psychologist recently explained it to me in a good way. He said that there is a tendency for their world to contract. Well, we must work on gently expanding their world.

That's what I want to help you do with this book, which is drawn extensively from my lectures.

Temple Talks...

about Autism and Sensory Issues

The Importance of Stretching and Choices

When I was 15, I had the opportunity to go to my aunt's ranch, and I was afraid to go. My mother gave me a big choice that has always stuck with me: I could go for one week or stay all summer. But staying home was not an option. I ended up loving the ranch and stayed all summer. It is important to stretch. I talked to another mom with a child in a similar situation. Her child was afraid to go to sleep-away camp. He stretched, he went to the sleep-away camp anyway, and he loved it. At my boarding school, they would not allow me to become a recluse in my room. Every Friday was movie night, and in the evening I got anxious and wanted to stay in my room. The headmaster, Mr. Patey, gave me a choice. I could be the projectionist of the movie or sit in the audience. I decided to become the projectionist. He gave me a choice. It is important to break down these barriers.

Must-Learn Basic Skills to Function in Society

Another important issue is politeness. I see too many kids today who are not learning basic skills, such as how to shake hands and say please and thank you. Their parents do too much talking for them. Due to slow attention shifting, children with autism are often slow to respond. Teachers and parents must wait and give the child time to respond and use his/her words. Children need to learn the simple rules of society. What disturbs me is that the tendency to overprotect children is often most apparent on the very mild end of the spectrum.

When I go to a gifted conference, I see the same kind of geeky, shy little kids going down a path that will lead to a successful career. One of the problems is that there is almost no overlap between the world of autism and the gifted world. When I check out the book table at the gifted conference, I notice there is almost no overlap in the books, and there really should be. I even went to a gifted conference social seminar. I thought, "Wait a minute: This sounds like an autism meeting."

1950s Upbringing Taught Social Skills

I will tell you how my 1950s upbringing really helped me. I went to college with a lot of kids who, today, would be labeled as having autism or Asperger's syndrome, and they are all employed. One reason for this is that in the 1950s and 1960s social skills were emphasized and taught to every child. They began the teaching with such things as turn taking during conversations and activities such as board games. Being on time was particularly important. We all learned that, and those are good rules to bear in mind.

There were some family activities I didn't like. I thought church was boring, but the rest of the family wanted to go, so I had to sit through it, not disrupt the service, and wear clothes I hated. Sometimes you have to do things other people want to do, which gets back to the fundamental concept of turn taking.

Desensitization to Loud Sounds

Fortunately, the church did not trigger sensory issues for me. If it had been a place that blasted rock-and-roll music, it would not have worked for me. It would have been too overwhelming. However, let's say that the family wanted to go to a church with loud music. Sometimes a child with autism can learn to tolerate a loud sound if he/she has some control over it. Perhaps the child could go into a sound booth and adjust the volume, and control the sound. Obviously, this would be done during rehearsals, and you would need understanding clergy. Another option would be to allow the child to wear headphones. Encourage the child to wear headphones around his/her neck and put them on only when the sound is unbearable. Headphones or earplugs MUST be off for at least half the day. Wearing headphones all the time will make sound oversensitivity worse, so save the headphones for the loudest places.

Use Teachable Moments

It is also essential to give clear instructions when a child does the wrong thing. If we were at the store and I grabbed some candy, my mother would calmly say, "Put it back, we're not buying candy today," and that is how she'd give me the instruction. She never said "no" or "stop it." If I twirled my fork in the air, she would say, "Put it on your plate." If I started to take a turn too quickly in a game she would say, "Wait for your sister to take a turn." There are many of these "teachable moments" every day. Being rude was not tolerated. I remember one time, my sister and I were laughing about how Aunt Bella's bosoms bounced up and down like horse feed bags. My mother said to us, "If Bella hears that, you're going to be grounded for a week." This is an example of really rude talk and bad table manners. We learned it was wrong.

Consistent Discipline is Essential

There was also consistent discipline between home and school. This is important to maintain. My mother and third grade teacher, who was the head teacher at the elementary school, were on the same page. There was a very simple rule for temper tantrums: no television for one night. If I threw a temper tantrum at school, Mrs. Dietsch would call home. When I got home, my mother would say, very matter-of-factly, "Mrs. Dietsch called today, so there will be no *Howdy Doody* show tonight." That was the rule. If I threw a fit, she'd put me in my room. After I calmed down, she would say, "Thank you for calming down, but no television tonight." I was angry, but I learned quickly what I could and could not get away with. Now, it's probably no iPad or no video game, but you take it away for just one night if the child misbehaves. My mother never yelled at me during a tantrum that she would take the TV away. She always waited for me to calm down. Never take away something that can turn into a career, such as art supplies or a musical instrument.

Teaching Interaction with Others

You have to learn social skills. I have taught so many kids how to shake hands using the right amount of pressure. My brother, sisters, and I learned how to interact with others by being hosts and hostesses at my mother's dinner parties. We had to greet the guests, take their coats, and serve them snacks. That is something any family can do. Almost all families have parties, order food in restaurants, or go shopping. If you are in a low-income situation, you could go to the local McDonald's and buy something from the dollar menu, but each child must go up to the counter and order the drink or snack he or she wants. One bad thing about kids today is that they are not participating in enough outdoor play or free play, during which they get together and learn to negotiate with other kids. Even non-autistic kids today don't know how to do free play, an activity that should be reintroduced into society.

I had an interesting talk with an organic farmer who had 10- and 11-year-old children spend a week at her walnut orchard and sleep in tents. No electronic screens were allowed. She said the kids, especially the boys, moped around for two days because they didn't have any video games. After going through two days of video game withdrawal, she said a switch flipped and the kids discovered that climbing trees was actually really fun. They often begged to come back the following year. We have to get back to more free play.

Eccentricity and Good Careers

It is okay to be eccentric. It is not okay to be rude or dirty. There is a difference. Do not try to de-geek the geek. Yesterday, I met a lady with a beautiful pink Hello Kitty outfit on. Yes, it was eccentric, but she looked very nice. At school last week, we were eating before class, and I saw a lady with lovely pink hair. It was beautifully done. That is fine; it is okay to be eccentric. However, you cannot be a slob. Figure 1 shows the guys at the Jet Propulsion Lab, and there is one who is probably close

to my age. What would happen to the junior version of him today? Would he get to have a fun job in which he's the navigator for the Mars Rover? Or would he be playing video games in a basement somewhere? This really worries

Credit: Reuters

Figure 1

me. I have made a point of being involved in the technology community. They need to reach out to gifted kids who have been labeled as being on the autism spectrum. One human resources manager said she knew that many engineers and programmers were on the spectrum but they did not like to talk about it.

There is a labor shortage in Silicon Valley. Too many kids who are smart in math are not getting their talents developed. I go to gifted conferences, autism conferences, cattle activities, and meat plant activities, and there are a lot of older, skilled trades and maintenance people in the plants who are on the autism spectrum. These are good jobs, in which one person had enough social skills to survive three plant owners and still keep his job. In fact, changing plants for these folks may be a bad idea. I knew a guy who worked for years in a shop in the maintenance department. He was brilliant with electronics, and when the company moved him to another plant, it was a disaster. He should have been left in the original plant, because he had a fight with the new boss. It was a real disaster, and he couldn't handle the change without help.

Learning to Control Anger

How did I deal with aggression? In ninth grade, I was kicked out of high school for fighting. Kids teased me, and I responded with aggression. I had to switch to crying. If you are angry, and feeling aggressive, sometimes you just have to try to do this. Crying is what National Aeronautics and Space Administration (NASA) scientists did when the shuttle was shut down. It was the saddest thing I had ever seen. On *60 Minutes* they walked away from the camera to avoid being filmed crying. I talked with two retired NASA scientists who had grandchildren on the autism spectrum. Yeah, they said that one-half of the people at NASA were probably on the autism spectrum.

A Rule System I Still Use

There is a rule system I still live with. I took all the rules of society and put them into four categories. First, if you want a civilized society, you cannot do really bad things like shoot people, burn down buildings, rob banks, and activities like that. You just cannot do those things and have a civilized society. Next, you have courtesy rules, which help people get along. Then you have things that are illegal but not necessarily bad. There are some ways to get around stupid school rules, which fall into this category as well. Finally, there are sins of the system, which have draconian penalties.

For example, after September 11, 2001, travelers have had to behave at airports. The World Trade Center attacks moved airports into the sin-of-the-system category. There have also been children who have done something stupid and been placed on the sex offenders list. If you're a sex offender in America, you get a GPS device secured to your ankle and your picture is placed on a horrible Web site.

These are examples of sins of the system, and you do not mess with sins of the system. This is something I figured out in high school. The reason I call them sins of the system is because something that is a sin of the system in America may not be a sin of the system in another country.

Here is another example of a sin of the system. In this country, I am allowed to criticize the president. I am not allowed to threaten him. There is a difference. Criticism is fine. I can say I hate his policies or love them, but I cannot threaten him. In another country, if I called the head of the country stupid, I could go to jail. That is what I mean by "sin of the system." The rules are different in various societies, whereas the first two categories tend to be more or less the same in different societies.

Dealing with Sensory Issues

The topic I want to address more specifically in this book is sensory issues. Sensory issues occur in conjunction with many different diagnostic labels, such as autism, dyslexia, attention deficit hyperactivity disorder (ADHD), and head injuries. The problem with a lot of these labels is that they are not precise enough. People treat them as if they are precise, as if they were receiving a diagnosis of tuberculosis, but they are not precise. In fact, according to the fifth edition of the Diagnostic and Statistical Manual of Mental Disorders (DSM 5), autism now covers a huge spectrum of people, from computer programmers in Silicon Valley and Einstein (who could not speak until age three) to those who are severely handicapped. In my opinion, removing all the diagnostic criteria about speech delay from the new DSM was a bad idea. I also think the American Psychiatric Association planned to call most cases of Asperger's syndrome in which there is no speech delay a social communication disorder, but that is not happening today because, unfortunately, there is no funding for it.

So, let's talk about my sensory issues and how they affected me. When I was a little kid, loud sounds hurt my ears. As you may know, sensory problems can vary from mild to extremely debilitating. One child may have a problem with sensitive hearing, while another may have problems with sensitive vision, such as being bothered by fluorescent lights; another may not tolerate certain smells.

But there is one basic principle. A lot of these things are tolerated much better if the child initiates them; for example, if he turns on the sound. Let's take microphone feedback; that can be a bad one for all of us. A child might be throwing a fit because he sees a microphone and is afraid it will squeal. So, if you hand him the microphone, walk over to the speaker, and have it make a sound, then he may back off. When he controls the initiation of the sound he/she may learn to tolerate it better.

Auditory Processing Problems

You can test a child's hearing and find that the auditory threshold—the ability to hear a faint sound—is normal, but that tells you absolutely nothing about auditory detail, the ability to hear hard consonant sounds. My speech teacher would hold up a cup and say "cup," and then she would say "cu-p," where she'd slow down and enunciate the hard consonants so I could hear them. When grown-ups talked really fast, it sounded like gibberish. In fact, I used to think grown-ups had their own special language. There are some individuals whose hearing may fade in and out like a bad mobile phone. And keep in mind that when a child gets tired, all of these problems get worse.

There are also different types of speech delay. I had trouble getting my speech out. Another kid might actually have a lot of speech and yak out all this echolalia and whole movie scripts, but he doesn't know what they mean. So you have different types of speech problems here, and you have to be aware of them and treat them differently.

Attention-Shifting Slowness

Another problem is attention-shifting slowness. Let's say a cellphone goes off in the room during one of my lectures. It attracts my attention, and it takes me much longer to shift back to something else, because I have attention-shifting slowness.

A study was conducted with a special device that tracks eye movement (Figure 2). Notice how many times non-autistic people look back and forth between the eyes. Autistic kids are looking at the mouth. They don't even know why they should be looking at the eyes. The eyes are not talking to them. However, one of the reasons they look at the mouth

Credit: Ami Klin

Figure 2

is because they may not hear very well. They are trying to lip-read and figure out what is being said. Look how many times the white lines, which show the eye movements of a normal person, went back and forth. The gray line, which tracked the eye movement of a person with autism, never shifted. This really shows attention-shifting slowness.

If you are working with a child with very severe sensory problems, it is important to watch out for clipping. Let me explain. If I said, "Tommy, hang up your coat," a child with severe sensory problems might hear only the word coat, because the first part of the sentence got clipped due to poor attention shifting. It took him that long to shift his attention to what you said. To get around this, you might want to first say, "Tommy, I need to ask you to do something." Now the channel is open, so you can go on to say, "Hang up your coat."

Visual Image Fragmentation

Other individuals may have problems in which visual images fragment and break up. I have looked at message boards on the Internet, and found one person who wrote that he had Picasso vision. Many of Picasso's paintings might have been influenced by some kind of visual-processing problem. Similarly, if you look at a picture from Oliver Sacks's book, *Migraine*, you will see that some of these visual-processing abnormalities resemble those that occur during a migraine headache. I don't have visual problems. This is where the sensory stuff is so variable.

What are some signs something is wrong with a kid's visual system? There may be lots of finger flicking in front of the eyes, and he or she may tilt the head to look out the corners of the eyes. One surprising cue is that often, children who have visual issues are terrified of escalators because they can't tell when to get on and off. The big one, however, is old-fashioned, 60-cycle fluorescent lights because kids with visual sensory issues can see them flicker. Now, thankfully, LEDs are starting to replace these fluorescents, and it's good riddance to those old 60-cycle lights.

If your child has an eye exam, often you are not going to find much because the problem is in the visual cortex. The issue is a large area at the back of the brain that assembles the image. This area has four types of circuits: shape, color, motion, and texture. These circuits must work together to form an image. In vision research, this is called the binding problem. Nobody really knows how it works, but in people with visual sensory issues, something is wrong with the visual cortex. Head injuries can also cause images to break up, and in some developmental disorders, a person might use the color circuits first, before he or she sees the shape.

In fact, if you want to read descriptions of some of these problems, there are some great books out there, such as *Carly's Voice*, by Arthur Fleischmann; *How Can I Talk If My Lips Don't Move?: Inside My Autistic Mind*, by Tito Rajarshay Mukhopadhyay; and *The Reason I Jump: The Inner Voice of a Thirteen-Year-Old Boy with Autism*, by Naoki Higashida.

Visual Reading Problems

If you ask a child who is fully verbal and having trouble learning to read, "Do you ever see the print jiggle on a page?" and the answer is *yes,* there is a problem with the visual system, and fluorescent lights will be especially problematic. I want to emphasize this does NOT explain all reading problems, but a subset of children may be helped by the procedures described in this section.

Here are some simple things you can do to help this type of visual problem. You can put an old-fashioned incandescent light—if you can still get one —next to the child's desk or put the child's desk next to a window. An LED light might work as well. The child could also try wearing a hat. An important thing to note is that if you are using computers, you should make sure you only use phones, laptops, and tablets. The other kinds of flat panels and old fashioned TV-type screens are terrible. Some of them have fluorescent lights that flicker inside them.

Try printing the child's homework on gray, tan, or pastel paper. This helps many kids. Let the child pick the color that works for him or her. Some individuals have been helped by the use of Irlen colored lenses.

It may help to make a trip to a local office supply store and experiment with pale pinks, lavenders, and tan-colored paper. Try every pale-colored paper the store has. Trying on pale pink, lavender, blue gray, or tan sunglasses may also be helpful. I had a student who bought some pink sunglasses that helped stop the print from jiggling.

Problems with Sensory Research

If you look at the research, you'll find that many studies have conflicting results. The problem with many of these kids with sensory issues is that there are so many subgroups. For instance, one child may have a visual-processing problem; another child may not. However, you can experiment with colored glasses and colored paper at very little cost. I have seen many people helped by this simple intervention. I was talking to the mother of a partially verbal little girl who could tolerate only five minutes of shopping in a large, busy store. After getting some little pink glasses, she could tolerate an hour of shopping in the same large store.

Difficult to Screen Out Background Stimulation

Having severe sensory problems means that a person has to apply extreme effort to screen out background noise. Often, such people need frequent breaks. They may need to either look at something or hear something. They are not able to do both things at once. People with severe visual problems are usually auditory thinkers, meaning they think best with their ears. Let them record and listen to their lessons, and they will do much better.

Environmental Enrichment Sensory Therapy

Scientists have learned a lot about the brain. In a new sensory study from the University of California-Irvine, Drs. Woo and Leon studied kids with autism and delayed speech, aged 4–12 years. This did not include kids with Asperger's syndrome and no speech delay. They did a controlled study, and one-half of the kids received sensory treatment, and the other half of the kids were controls. All of the children, including the controls, continued their current treatments, whether it was ABA (Applied Behavior Analysis), speech therapy, or something else. The children who received additional sensory treatment underwent a half-hour session in the morning and a half-hour session in the afternoon that included all kinds of sensory stimulations. Two sensory systems, such as touch and smell, were always stimulated simultaneously. Eight different aromatherapy scents were used.

What is important about this study is the novelty of the stimulation. Novelty is key in these instances: Have children walk on different kinds of floor surfaces, smell different odors, and do activities in front of mirrors (e.g., put things in jars while looking in a mirror). Novelty—always changing the stimuli used—is very important. The other key is engaging more than one sense in each activity. For instance, in the study music was incorporated in the therapy sessions and paired with either tactile (touch) or smell stimuli. Many activities involved touch, such as drawing patterns on the child's back with a finger or rubbing with warm and cold spoons.

Another useful aspect of this study is that it employed inexpensive items most people already have in their homes. Almost everyone has a mirror, and you could easily have children do things like walk on a rug and then walk on a hard floor. If you don't have either of those surfaces, you could put a piece of cardboard down and have children walk on that. You don't need a whole lot of expensive items, and the scientists achieved some very good results. The kids showed significant improvements in speech and behavior.

There were also improvements in speech and behavior among the older kids (8, 9, and 12 years old). This was true both on the parents' assessment, which was not blind, and on the professional assessment, conducted by a researcher who was completely blind to the treatment. This is pretty exciting stuff to me, as it helps prove that sensory issues are real. Again, one of the keys to the treatment was variation of stimulation; it must have novelty. You can read more about this important study in the appendix.

Brain Research Validates Sensory Issues

Sensory problems are real. There has been a lot of research showing that there are differences in the brain. One study I read shows that the fear center is activated when the person experiences the dreaded sensory stimulation. As a personal example, when I was younger, I remember loud sounds hurting my ears. But there is also a real fear element involved that many don't know about. The entire nervous system is aroused—overaroused, even, when the stimulation occurs—and you get a much bigger startle response than normal.

Brain May Be Either More Thinking or More Social

Other research has shown that in autism some of the social circuits in the frontal cortex are not hooked up. I think we need to start looking at a lot of personality traits as if they were variable, like the volume on a music mixing board. For instance, you could make the anxiety trait stronger, or you could make it milder. One person may have a brain that has developed more for thinking and another person has a brain more developed for socializing. There is a range that reflects normal variation in personality. When does normal variation become an abnormality? When do geeks and nerds become kids with mild autism? There is no black and white dividing line. Interestingly, I have been to a number of different companies in Silicon Valley, and, boy, can I tell you: There is no dividing line. Mild autism is everywhere. In fact, when you put two of those mildly autistic computer scientists together and they marry, they can sometimes have severely autistic kids. The genetics are complex, but when both parents have autism traits, the chances of having a child with severe autism might increase. The older technology companies have many families with autistic grandchildren.

When you hear, see, speak, or think about a word, different parts of the brain are turned on, and circuits connect these different brain centers. This is where the abnormalities occur, in the communication between different parts of the brain. You can see this in Figure 3.

My Brain Scans

Figure 4 is a picture of my head. And here is the connectome for humans. A connectome is a comprehensive map of neural connections in the brain, and may be thought of as its "wiring diagram" of the fiber bundles that are the "interoffice" connections in the brain connecting up different departments. This image was taken by Walter Schneider at the University of Pittsburgh with state-of-the-art, high-definition diffusion-tensor imaging, which is able to track individual cable bundles of white matter circuits that go between the different parts of the brain. This research was originally paid for by the Defense Department

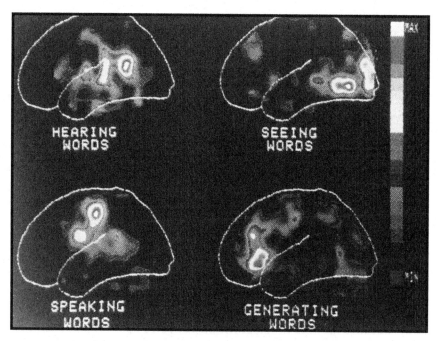

Figure 3

Figure 4

to study head injuries in veterans; however, it could also be a great diagnostic tool for people with developmental problems. Wouldn't it be nice to be able to determine exactly where a speech problem is? The tiny single fibers are single axons, which go all the way across the brain and form cable bundles (Figure 5).

On the right of Figure 5 is the normal circuit. That is the circuit for what I will call, "speak what you see," which goes from the visual cortex of the brain up into the language area. Now look at my circuit on the left. I've got a whole lot of extra bushes in the "speak what you see" area that go across the entire brain, meaning that when you put a keyword in, I get pictures. I sort of have a language space for a keyword system that works like Google Images.

Now, you might ask, "At what point does an extra bush become abnormal?" There is no black and white dividing line on some of these issues because they are developmental. The price I pay for all of my extra bushes is that I get less bandwidth for "speak what I see." In other words, I have fewer fibers with which to tell what I see. I had delayed speech and I had trouble getting my words out. I'm going to hypothesize that in a child with echolalia, this circuit is going to be more normal and there will be problems in another circuit involved with understanding the meaning of speech.

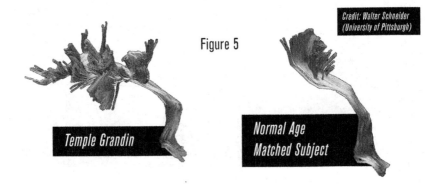

Figure 5

Credit: Walter Schneider
(University of Pittsburgh)

Temple Grandin

Normal Age
Matched Subject

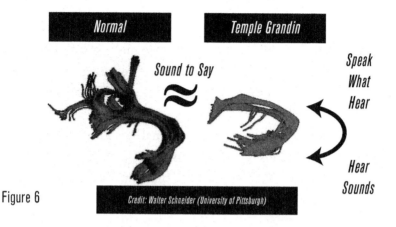

Figure 6

Credit: Walter Schneider (University of Pittsburgh)

Figure 6 represents the cable bundle in the brain for "speak what you hear." You can see from the image on the right that I have a little tiny shrimp there, much smaller than most people. I am definitely not an auditory learner, although many people are.

Build and Encourage the Child's Strength

Figure 7 is a picture a young child drew in perspective, when very young. It is basic, but the perspective at that age shows great promise. It's important to build on those strengths and abilities. I often get asked, "When do strengths start to appear?" In most kids, they begin to appear around the third or fourth grade (7 to 9 years). That is when my drawing

Figure 7

ability became evident. Drawing ability will show up at that time, as will mathematical ability. It's important to make sure kids with mathematical ability continue to move ahead because if they are made to do the same math repeatedly, they will become bored, and behavior problems may develop.

Another issue that arises in kids with mathematical ability is that, today, teachers want kids to show their work. I'll tell you right now, that's not how some of these kids are capable of doing it. They think differently. However, I would certainly still take some precautions against cheating to make sure they haven't written the answers down somewhere (e.g., under their shirt).

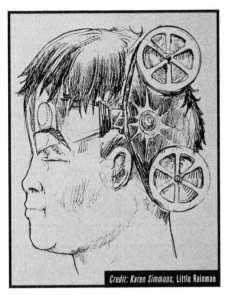

Credit: Karen Simmons, Little Rainman

Figure 8

My mind works like Google Images. This is a picture of a movie projector in the head from the book *Little Rainman: Autism—Through the Eyes of a Child* (Figure 8). That is exactly how I think: in pictures.

I have had teachers say to me, "How can I get the pictures out of a kid's head?" You can't. You don't want to. That is how they think. Being a visual thinker has really helped me in my work with livestock, because I can test run equipment in my mind. Until I started asking people about how they thought, I assumed that everyone test ran equipment in their minds. I didn't know my thinking was different. After talking to others, I realized it was different. And I realized how this difference has helped me.

My mother always encouraged my ability in art and I used my visual abilities in my work designing livestock facilities. See Figure 9 for an example of my work.

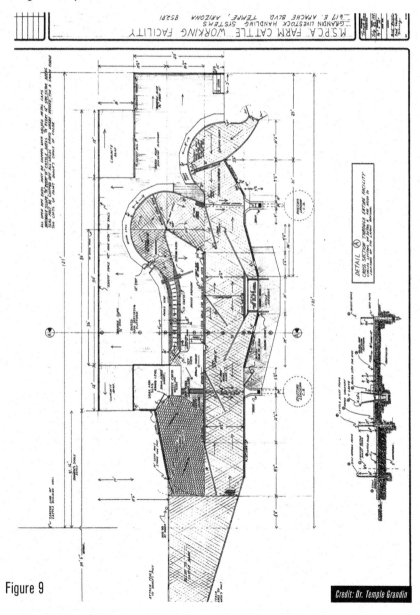

Figure 9

Forming Concepts

So, how do you form a concept when you have all these specific pictures floating around in your head? One young man sent me a picture to show how he makes boxes in his head like a series of file folders (Figure 10). He sorts specific pictures into categories to form a concept. This is also called bottom-up thinking, in which concepts are formed by taking specific pictures from memory and sorting them into different boxes. For example, I can sort many different specific cats and dogs I have seen in the past into different boxes. I can also sort rude versus polite behavior into different boxes. For me, behavior concepts have to be taught by specific examples. Let's say I spat on the side-walk; my mother would say that's rude. I had to learn the rude concept with several different specific examples, such as shoving in line or telling someone they are stupid.

Credit: Karen Simmons, Little Rainman

Figure 10

Another thing I teach parents and educators about these kids is, instead of screaming "no!," give simple instructions. Let's say I ate mashed potatoes with my hands. My mother wouldn't scream "no"; she would say, "Use the fork." She would calmly and simply give the instruction instead of screaming "no." That's the way to do it. Concepts are formed with specific examples. This is a very important idea to get across to you.

Gradually Learning My Thinking was Different

I realized my thinking was different when I asked a speech therapist at a conference to think about a church steeple. I was shocked to find out that she and many other people think of a vague, generalized pointy thing. I see only specific steeples I have seen in the past; there is no generalized pointy thing. My concept of a steeple is based on lots of specific examples I put in a file folder in my mind labeled "steeple." I have another file folder in my mind labeled "cellphone tower." Now I'm seeing a series of individual normal cellphone towers. I'm seeing the Hilton Hotel in Fort Collins, which has them on the roof. I'm seeing these stupid fake trees they put the towers on. The cellphone tower images are specific. My images come up in my mind like Google Images. How about childhood images of steeples or local steeples in Fort Collins? How about famous steeples? I sort them into different categories: Famous ones, local ones, cathedral types, and chapel types. I start making steeple categories. I have one big file folder for all steeples, and then I make subcategories for different types of steeples. That's the way my brain works naturally.

In order to make these subcategories, I must be exposed to many different steeples. This is why it is so important for these children to get out and do a lot of things. It is important to fill the mind with many images they can look at. Imagine an autistic child's brain starting as a vast, empty Internet, equipped with a good Google search engine. You need to fill it up with Web pages so the child has lots of specific examples he or she can search in the future. I used to jokingly say I have a huge visual thinking circuit that goes deep into my visual cortex (Figure 11). Well, it turns out I do. Not the biggest visual thinking circuit that exists; I'm sure there are art professors with bigger ones. But I am probably in the top 20%. You can see the circuit goes all the way back into the visual cortex. The brain scan in Figure 12 shows why my ability in algebra is

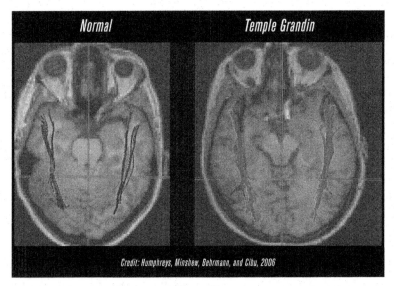

Figure 11

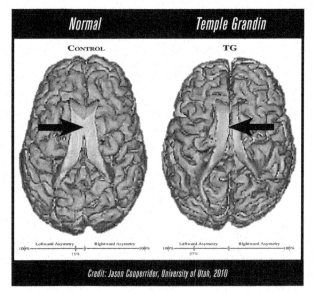

Figure 12

so terrible. In this figure, the indicated area is full of water, or cerebral spinal fluid, and you can see that it pretty well trashed the left parietal area. I have really bad working memory.

Worried That the Educational System Will Sideline Smart Kids

I am very concerned that with all the emphasis on algebra today, a lot of us visual thinkers are going to get screened out. So how did I manage to get through college without this ability? In 1967, finite math was a fad. Now, algebra is a fad. In 1967, finite math—matrices, probability, and statistics—was a required class across the country, and, with tutoring, I was able to do it. Thank goodness it wasn't algebra. I got decent grades in finite math.

Different Kinds of Minds

One of the most important things you have to understand is that all people think differently, and this affects how they learn and the types of jobs they should have. You get kids who are labeled as having autism, Asperger's syndrome, dyslexia, ADHD, or any other condition in which people tend to have uneven skills, meaning they are good at one thing and bad at something else. I am what's called an object visualizer, meaning I am a photorealistic visual thinker who thinks in photorealistic pictures. Someone like that may have trouble with algebra. Another kind of visual spatial thinker is the pattern thinker. These people have a mathematical or an engineering mind. They think in patterns, and they often have trouble reading. They should be allowed to study more advanced math and be introduced to computer programming.

In my book, *The Autistic Brain*, I present scientific research that shows these two kinds of visual thinking really exist. My kind of visual thinking uses the circuits in the brain that tell what something is. In your brain, you have "what" circuits and "where" circuits. My brain uses the "what-is-something" circuits. Mathematicians use the "where-am-I-located-in-space" circuits. That is the mathematician's mind, the mind of the engineer. Brain scan studies referenced in the appendix show there are two types of visual thinking and a third type, which is verbal thinking. Let me tell you that the industry needs the visual thinkers. When I found out why the Fukushima nuclear power plant burned up, I couldn't believe it. They made a visualization mistake that was so obvious to me. When you live next to the sea, it is not a very good idea to put the emergency generators for your cooling system in a non-waterproof basement. If they had bought some watertight doors from a shipbuilding company, this would not have happened. I can't design a nuclear reactor, but that is not a mistake I would have made. I would have visualized the water drowning the generators and emergency pumps. The mathematical mind that thinks in patterns, the mind that designs the reactor, does not see the water filling the basement.

Another kind of mind is the verbal fact mind. The different kinds of thinking types tend to show up in elementary school, not at age three. There are some exceptions, but you usually don't see these thinking types in three year olds. In first grade, my brain's visual thinking was not obvious. It was during third or fourth grade when my art ability became obvious.

What can you look for in kids to determine the kind of thinkers they are? Children with my kind of mind tend to draw a lot of

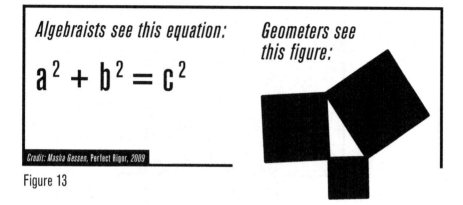

Algebraists see this equation:

$$a^2 + b^2 = c^2$$

Geometers see this figure:

Credit: Masha Gessen, Perfect Rigor, 2009

Figure 13

pictures. Both the pattern thinkers and visual thinkers like to play with LEGOs. Word thinkers usually don't care much for LEGO or drawing, and pattern thinkers are good at math if you don't ruin them by asking them to show their work. There are two ways you can do math. You can do it the verbal way, or you can do it the more visual-spatial way. (Figure 13).

Credit: Robert Lang, 2006

Figure 14

I would like to give you a glimpse of a mind that is not mine (Figure 14). This is from the brain of a pattern-thinking mathematician. This praying mantis is made from a single sheet of folded paper, with no cuts, and no tape. The folding pattern is seen in the background. I look at that and think, "Wow, that is definitely not my mind." Here are some origami stars some kids gave me at a convention (Figure 15). They show the same kind of thinking.

Figure 15

Learning to Drive

What about driving? It will take longer for kids with autism and sensory issues to learn how to drive. One good thing I did was to spend a year driving on easy roads before I started driving on busy freeways. Practice, practice, and more practice helps avoid the multitasking problems many people experience in learning to drive a car. It eventually leads to the operation of the car becoming automatic before the child begins to drive in traffic. I actually learned to drive at my aunt's ranch. It was three miles to the mailbox, and three miles back, and I used that to practice, and make the driving skills automatic. Make sure you, too, can find a safe place in which to understand the process. There is an old military base outside of San Francisco. The town is still there, but it is vacant. This is a great place to learn how to drive, as are large parking lots, open fields, and dirt roads. These are safe places where kids can practice driving before they advance to scarier roads, such as freeways and places with denser traffic.

Special Interests I Could Share with Peers Which Were Refuges from Bullying

When I was being bullied and teased in high school what really helped me were all the hands-on activities. The only times I was not bullied and teased were when I was engaging in special-interest activities such as horse riding, building model rockets, and working with electronics. I can't emphasize enough the importance of getting kids involved in specialized interests. One of the worst things schools have done is to take out hands-on classes such as art, music, cooking, sewing, woodworking theater, metal shop, welding, and auto shop. There are a whole lot of jobs available for auto mechanics, electricians, and a lot of other skilled trades. It takes smart people to do these things.

Understanding Abstract Concepts

Photo Courtesy of Dr. Temple Grandin

Figure 16

How do you think about really abstract stuff when you think completely in pictures? When I was a young child, one of my first language assignments was to learn the Lord's Prayer. What is the power and the glory? Figure 16 is my picture for the power and the glory. We have a rainbow (which shows up as a white streak in the black and white photo) with an electric tower at the base of the rainbow. That's the power and the glory. This picture was not Photoshopped. It is real.

Bottom Up Thinking

I would like to review bottom-up thinking. This is a very important concept. All my thinking uses specific examples to create concepts, which is the opposite to how most people think. Most people form a hypothesis first; they then tend to overgeneralize and try to make all the specific data fit the hypothesis. I create the hypothesis by piecing together the data. It is bottom-up, not top-down thinking, and everything is learned with specific examples. Concepts are made up of specific examples, so let's play games with categorizing objects. That way, children can learn things like color, shape, "bigger than," and "smaller than." I could sort these objects by

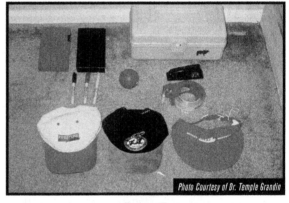

Photo Courtesy of Dr. Temple Grandin

Figure 17

color, and I could sort out the rectangular objects, as you see in Figure 17. Some objects are going to be in more than one category, but that's something that is important to learn. One object might be both red and rectangular. The brains of children with autism pick out the details; people in this spectrum are often very good at details.

I was very happy to hear that the big technology company SAP is now hiring people with autism to debug software, because autistic people are very good at details. If you show slides of these letters (Figure 18), people with autism will pick out small letters more quickly than they will pick out large letters. That is what happens when you are looking at the details.

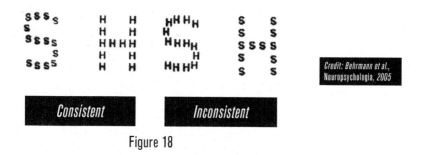

Credit: Behrmann et al.,
Neuropsychologia, 2005

Consistent   **Inconsistent**

Figure 18

Is Autistic Learning Simply Scripting?

A lot of people ask me, "Is autistic learning just memorizing and script-ing?" Yes, in the beginning, it can be. When I was in high school, other kids used to call me a tape recorder. I could understand why they called me a workhorse, but not a tape recorder. The reason was because I always used the same scripts; however, if you get children out and have them do things, you fill the "Internet" that is inside their heads with "Web pages," giving them more examples from which to draw. This is why it is important to have them get out and do things. Think of the brain as an Internet. As more information is loaded into the brain, the Internet fills up, and the brain acts as a type of Google search engine in order to find things.

Teaching Number Concepts and Position Words

It is also important to teach number concepts and generalization. Be-gin by counting a variety of objects: two cars, two pencils, two glasses of water. The concept of a number applies to many different things. You could begin teaching fractions by cutting up an apple and then move on to number lines. It is important to understand that you can have one-half or one-fourth of something. Children must understand these basic concepts.

How does one teach a position word that tells where something is? Common position words are up, down, in, on, under, above, and below. I talked to one mother whose child thought the word "up" only applied to stairs. To avoid this, you must apply the word to many different situations. The plane went up in the air. I put the cereal up in the cabinet. The dog jumped up. I walked down the stairs. The plane went down and landed. I put a cup down. I lie down on the bed. You must use several different examples to teach concepts such as "up," "down," "in," "on," and "beside." Otherwise, it is easy for the child to think the word only applies to one definition.

If you are teaching a child with echolalia, who repeats things such as movie scripts, he has to be taught that words have meaning. He or she may sing a cereal commercial to you in the morning because it is associated with food. You should immediately give him/her the same brand of cereal. Then he/she will start to learn that the words being scripted have meaning. In that case, you should start teaching nouns. If the child says "juice," give him or her the juice so the child learns that the word has meaning. Start teaching nouns with flashcards where a picture of an object such as an apple appears on the same side of the card next to the written word *apple*.

Interested in Things

When I was a child, I was a lot more interested in looking at pictures of things than I was in looking at pictures of people. I think a brain can be made more cognitive or more social. We need people who are interested in things. Tesla, the man who invented the power plant, would be labeled autistic today. We need to have people who like things.

Socialization Through Shared Activities Such as Art, Music, Robotics, or Mechanics

I cannot emphasize enough the importance of social interactions through shared interests, such as school, clubs, and activities. I am often asked about public versus private schools. I have found that so much depends on the particular school and situation. One mother I talked to said her child was in a band and another music activity at the local high school and was doing fine. For another child at a different school, everything was horrible due to bullying and no peers in a group with shared interests. Activities such as Future Farmers of America (FFA) and other farm programs, boy and girl scouts, and maker community groups are wonderful. Maker community groups are really cool groups in which people get together and just make all kinds of things, such as three-dimensional images and robotics. There are all sorts of wonderful specialized activities. What if you live in a rural area? How about fixing broken lawnmowers? Recruit a retired mechanic to start a small engine repair class for kids in middle school. Middle school is the right age to get kids interested in things that can become a career.

You must show kids interesting things in order to get them interested. Today, there are serious problems with kids not being shown enough interesting things. Recently, I gave a lecture in a college class, and many students asked me, "How did you become interested in your passions?" I was exposed to cattle when I was in high school. You don't become interested in things you are not exposed to. This is one reason why all children must get out and become involved with a variety of activities.

The Importance of Categorizing Behavior Problems

It is important to categorize behavior problems. People tend to overgeneralize; they'll say, "What can you do for autism?" If the child is three with no speech, I can recommend early educational intervention. For an older child, I will need lots more information before I can give any recommendations. If you have a child who has severe autism and limited speech, you must figure out if the behavior problem is caused by sensory oversensitivity. Is the child screaming because a noise bothers her or because there is the threat of a scary noise? Does she see a microphone, and is scared it might make a noise? A hidden painful medical problem is another big issue. You must rule that out in individuals who are not able to talk.

You may have a verbally competent individual who has trouble processing rapid verbal information. For these children, you must talk more slowly so they can process the information more easily. Often, written instructions are better, because they enable children to process them at their own pace. I cannot remember long strings of verbal communications. I need to see it written down because I have difficulty remembering the correct order of a long sequence.

Have you determined that the problem is purely behavioral? You may have someone who cannot talk and is frustrated because he or she is unable to communicate. Some individuals who cannot talk do learn to type independently. For these people, it is important to use a tablet rather than a desktop or laptop computer because when you type on the virtual keyboard of a tablet, the print appears right next to the keyboard; there is no attention shift. With a laptop or desktop computer, the user must look up, and thus shift his or her attention back and forth. Often, individuals with severe autism are unable to make this shift, so it is important to use a tablet.

Maybe the person is behaving badly to get attention or to get out of doing something. You must figure out what is motivating the behavior.

There are some things that may require accommodation. For instance, some kids may need to be taken out of fire drills, or kept away from supermarkets because the sensory overload would be too much for them.

Environmental Enrichment Therapy

I hope this new study from the University of California will show we can improve some of these situations by exposing children to different sensory environments. Two stimuli, such as music and smell, should always occur simultaneously. You could also have children look in a mirror while putting pennies in a cup or perhaps some other activity that traverses the sensory systems.

To this day, I cannot tolerate scratchy clothes. I have found that even some cotton itches. I used to love wearing a certain brand of cotton pants; then the manufacturer cheapened them up, and I don't wear them anymore because they make me itch. They were 100% cotton, but I won't buy them because even after I washed them three times they were still scratchy. Some kids have a terrible time with handwriting. Those kids should be allowed to type. The fluorescent light issue is a real problem. Some kids have difficulty multitasking. I don't do a very good job of multitasking, and I have trouble with long strings of verbal instruction.

Going back to the study I was talking about earlier, you might also play some music while doing an activity, because one of the principles is engaging in a variety of things and stimulating two or more senses at a time without causing sensory overload. For instance, a child might walk on different kinds of flooring, such as a rug and a bare floor, while music is playing, smells are present, or he or she is in front of a mirror.

Figure 19

I loved mirrors as a kid; I was fascinated by them. We would go to my aunt's house, and I would run down a long hallway at the end of which was a large mirror, and watch myself get bigger as I approached. Figure 19 shows a child swinging on a swing. The researchers did not use a swing in this particular study because they were trying to keep costs down and limit themselves to things most people have in their homes, but some kids respond really well to slow swinging such as the kind you see here. Some kids also respond well to therapeutic horseback riding because it involves both rhythm and balancing.

The researchers also engaged activities that involved balancing. For a simple balancing activity, you could nail an 8 ft. 2 x 4 board to the floor and have the child walk on it. Figure 20 shows a boy with a weighted vest. To make this work, have the child wear the vest for about 20 minutes and then take it off for a while. The thing to remember about these sensory activities, especially when you are using single things repeatedly, is that they work for some children but not for others. So you have to try different things until you find what works. A key finding in the study was that using stimuli that kept changing was important. A common mistake in many sensory programs is always using the same thing. Try a weighted vest with aromatherapy scents that are constantly changing.

I think it is important to de-sensitize touch in small children so they will like hugging, or at least tolerate it without distress. This is another thing that was done in the California study. To do this, you could hug the child while he or she is listening

Photo Courtesy of Dr. Temple Grandin

Figure 20

to music or doing some other sensory activity. Touching is one of the easiest things you can do to desensitize. Remember: Tickle touches are alarming, and firm pressure is calming.

Hidden Medical Problems Cause Behavior Problems

One other important aspect we have to look at in these kids is medical issues in non-verbal individuals. Sometimes, what is causing bad behaviors is really the child having a reaction to pain that you do not know about. Let's look at hidden painful medical problems that can occur in a nonverbal person. Acid reflux is a big one. A child may be behaving badly because her stomach hurts. You may see an odd stretching behavior in children with acid reflux; stomach doctors call it saluting. The child puts his hands over his head because it helps relieve the pain. Treatment for acid reflex may provide relief. The downside is that doctors often say that it's just autism. No. If a child has acid reflux, it needs to be treated. How about constipation? How about urinary tract infections? There are simple tests for these conditions. Yeast infections, ear infections, a bad tooth—if you have a nonverbal individual who has been doing really well and then suddenly is doing terribly, you must consider the child has a hidden painful medical issue.

Deep-Pressure Reduced Anxiety

Figure 21 illustrates my squeezing machine. When I entered puberty, I started experiencing panic attacks from all the hormones. Exercise helped. The deep pressure from the squeeze machine also helped ease my anxiety. From looking at brain scans, I have since learned that my fear center is three times the size of normal fear centers. An enlarged amygdala occurs in a subgroup of people with autism. This tends to be a problem with visual thinkers. I have also seen this problem in non-autistic industrial designers

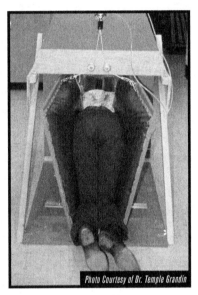

Photo Courtesy of Dr. Temple Grandin

Figure 21

and artists. A low dose of antidepressant medication really helped me with this. (See my book *Thinking in Pictures* for a complete description of my experiences with antidepressants.)

We should also talk about special diets. In some individuals, vitamin supplements and fish oil have been helpful. Some people have found that a weighted blanket helps them to sleep at night. It is also important to cut back on sugar. Drinking a gallon of soda every day is not good.

Family History

I have a typical family history. On my father's side, we have four generations of bankers. On my mother's side, we have a Massachusetts Institute of Technology–trained engineer who was the co-inventor of the
autopilot used in airplanes. We have a history of anxiety and depression
on both sides. On my mother's side, there is a lot of intellectual talent
and visual thinking. There are food allergies on my father's side, and
there are some Asperger's traits on both sides of the family. These are
continuous traits. The genetics are extremely complicated; this is not a
simple Mendelian inheritance.

Q&A

Questions and Answers with Temple

wanted to share with you some of the many questions I am asked and the answers I give. These are all questions I am asked very often, and I hope many of you will gain insights from my answers. I often reference my other books as an additional resource if I think they will help readers with more information on the relevant topic.

Enjoy!

General Sensory Questions

Q: My daughter is very sensitive to certain noises and sounds. It has gotten to the point that she doesn't even want to leave the house. What can we do?

A: She may be able to learn to tolerate the dreaded sounds if she has control of the exposure. There must be no sudden surprises. Try putting the bad sounds on a high-fidelity recording device where she controls the volume. Start at a very low volume. She may be afraid to leave the house because she fears getting her ears hurt by the sound.

(Additional resource: *The Autistic Brain*)

Q: My son, Max, is four years old and has been diagnosed with 'moderate to severe' autism. He is absolutely terrified of one of my co-workers, who also has a daughter in his class at school. Every time he sees my co-worker he screams, cries, throws things ... basically has a tantrum. She provided him with a treat every time she saw him and his wild behavior decreased, but it has once again greatly increased, although the response is much shorter lived. Obviously, my co-worker is distressed about this. Where do we go from here?

A: Could be there is a sensory reason involved.

Sometimes a child will avoid certain people, not because they have done anything bad to them but because they cause the child to experience sensory overload.

It could be the odor of the laundry soap they wash their clothes in, the overpowering smell of perfume; maybe they have a high-pitched voice (in some women) or carry cell phones with a high-pitched ringtone that hurts the child's ears.

Q: My son does not like getting wet, and has started throwing fits at bath time. Obviously, he needs to be able to bathe, but I cannot go through with this drama every night. Any suggestions would be greatly appreciated!

A: You may be able to desensitize him by letting him control how wet he gets. Try getting a shower nozzle with a hose he can hold and totally control. He could spray it on the wall first, and then gradually direct the spray onto himself.

Q: Temple, I heard you mention that some very young kids can be drawn out of autism and into the world around them more easily than others. Can you please elaborate?

A: I was referring to the severity of sensory problems. Children with less severe sensory problems can be pulled out of their autistic world more easily. Children with severe sensory problems have to be treated much more gently to prevent sensory overload. One has to be very careful not to overstimulate.

(Additional resource: *The Way I See It*)

Q: My son doesn't want anyone to touch one of his feet. He has even started hopping to avoid the floor. We have taken him to the doctor, and they can find no medical reason for his sensitivity. Do you have any experience with this kind of problem?

A: An occupational therapist trained in sensory integration may be able to help. Another possible way to desensitize the child's foot is deep-pressure massages or wrapping it in a bandage to provide gentle pressure for 30 minutes. Immediately after having the bandage removed, he may be able to tolerate having his foot touched. There are some children in whom this problem is true tactile defensiveness. In your child's case, it is likely to be attention seeking, since he hops so much.

(Additional resource: *The Way I See It* and *Thinking in Pictures*)

Q: We live in the city, and are close to a hospital. The problem is the noises that come from the ambulances coming and going. They are bothering our daughter with autism very much. How can she learn to ignore them?

A: Maybe you could desensitize her to ambulance sirens by having her play videos of them that she controls. Loud noises are better tolerated if the person with autism can turn them on and off. She could learn to play them at gradually increasing volume.

Q: My wife and I have a seven-year-old son who has Asperger's syndrome. My wife noticed signs at around 18 months, and his pediatrician at the time informally diagnosed him as having "high-functioning autism." He taught himself to read before the age of three and didn't speak more than about 20 words until he was reading. He had the words in his mind all along! He was officially diagnosed as having Asperger's syndrome in 2011. He is highly intelligent and has been accepted into the gifted and talented program at his elementary school. He's been mainstreamed through school, and the teachers and everyone involved in the school system have been just wonderful. He is very touch oriented, and loves to give hugs and hold hands. William likes to draw and build things. His latest project is a castle he's making out of a computer box. He has skylights, a satellite dish, a generator, and even a drawbridge. Everything to him is connected to electricity. When asked about why everything is connected to electricity, he says it's because that's how he sees it. You know more than anyone how the mind works, and that's what the question is about. I could write a book on the way he sees things; if I could only understand what he means most of the time. My wife and I are intelligent people, but he has an understanding of things that sometimes completely mystifies us. The question is, what can we as parents do to better understand him and his behaviors? He absolutely cannot tolerate a baby's cry, loud crowds, or loud environments. He will cover his ears and yell or hum, depending on the level of stimulation. Thank you for taking the time to read this and answer.

A: Thank you for your email regarding your son.

I have a few suggestions I think will help him. Try broadening his creativity and encourage it as much as possible. The fact that he made a castle out of a computer box shows his level of creative design capability. Work on developing his designs into something people will want. I wanted to draw horse heads all the time, but mother encouraged me to draw many different things. Start by suggesting he draw something associated with his fixation. In my case, being told to draw a horse's stable or saddle would still invoke an associated link back to horses. You need to work on de-sensitizing sounds. For instance, go into a store with florescent lighting, let him control how much exposure he gets to the sounds, lights, etc.

Another example would be to let your child pop balloons himself. Place a towel around a smoke detector and gradually let your child remove the towel to expose the sound. Let him be in control of the noise.

(Additional resources: *The Way I See It* and *Thinking in Pictures*)

Q: My daughter has SPD (sensory processing disorder) and is bothered by vision, especially reading text at school. What can we do to help her?

A: Signs of visual processing disorders are:

1. Child reports seeing the print on the page jiggle.

2. He/she may fear escalators, because they fear getting on or off.

This disorder can sometimes be improved by wearing pale-tinted colored glasses. You have to find the specific color that works for you. Try pale rose, light blue, tan, lavender, or yellow. If you have access to an Irlen provider, they may help you. Colored glasses from Irlen are costly. Often it is possible to find something that works by trying many different pale-tinted colored glasses. You should also try printing his pages on many different pale pastel-colored papers: tan, gray, lavender, and blue. Let the child pick the color.

Q: I have difficulty hearing people in crowds. Everyone else seems to be able to sit in large groups and focus on what one person is saying. I cannot tune out all of the other ambient noise. Do you experience anything like this? What do you do to get over it?

A: I also have trouble hearing when there is too much background noise. Hearing in a noisy restaurant is difficult. On the cell phone, I have to turn the volume up very loud. My hearing test was normal. This disorder is called auditory processing disorder or lack of phonological awareness. You may also have problems hearing hard consonant sounds. I cannot tell if a person said bat, cat, or pat. I have to figure out the word by its context. I often have to ask people to speak up. When I was a child, I had difficulty hearing people who were speaking fast. The hard consonant sounds dropped out and all I could hear were the vowels. There are some listening and auditory training CDs available, but I have no information on how well they work.

Q: My friend has Asperger's, and sometimes doesn't recognize me until I talk! Is this unusual?

A: Many people with Asperger's have a problem recognizing faces. I often fail to recognize people I have just met.

Q: My son has many sensory issues, and has not been able to learn to swim yet. He is nine years old. Could this be a sensory problem?

A: Problems with learning to swim may be due to poor coordination. You should consult an occupational therapist who is trained in autism.

Diagnosis

I get many questions on the different diagnoses related to autism. Here are a few examples.

Q: Are autism and sensory processing disorders the same?

A: People can have Asperger's or autism; they can also have sensory processing disorder. It is also possible to have sensory processing disorder with no Asperger's or autism. The core symptom of Asperger's and autism is problems with social communication, fixated interests, and repetitive behaviors. I know people who have sensory processing disorder with no symptoms of autism spectrum disorder.

Q: My brother is always in his own head, talking out loud about the stories in his mind. He loves to draw pictures and animation. My mother thinks he may have schizophrenia, due to the constant storytelling. I think he is just unique. What do you think?

A: When I was little I talked out loud and told stories to myself. I was allowed to do this at night in bed. His stories are NOT schizophrenia. I would encourage his interest in animation and motivate him to make many DIFFERENT characters. Maybe you could give him an assignment to make an animation movie. Build on his strength.

(Additional resources: *Thinking in Pictures, The Autistic Brain,* and *The Way I See It*)

Q: I have a son with autism who has many sensory issues. I also have a friend who suffered a head injury in a car accident. After the accident, that friend developed sensory issues as well. Do they both have SPD, and is it the same thing now?

A: Many people with head injuries get sensory processing disorders. In a head injury, problems occur due to circuits getting ripped. In a developmental disorder, the brain circuits grow the wrong way.

Q: How large a spectrum is there for degrees of autism? Does dyslexia fit in there?

A: Autism covers a very wide spectrum. It ranges from very severe, where many children are non-verbal and often have medical problems such as epilepsy, to the Silicon Valley genius. Other examples of people who had autism are Einstein, Mozart, and Van Gogh. Einstein could not talk until he was three years old. It is possible that dyslexia and autism can present together, however dyslexia can also present by itself.

(Additional resources: *Thinking in Pictures* and *The Way I See It*)

Q: What is the difference between autism and ADHD? Thank you!

A: Mild autism and ADHD have many similar traits. One way to find a good school is to talk to other parents. If you find a school by searching online, make sure you talk to parents who have sent their child to the school. Joining a local support group is another way of finding good resources, for both ADHD and autism.

Q: Where does the line lie between someone who is normal and someone who has autism?

A: There is no real dividing line between autism and normal. The computer you wrote your email on was designed by a brilliant person
who was socially awkward. A little autism or Asperger's is essential
to develop things such as computers.

(Additional resource: *The Autistic Brain*)

Q: Is autism genetic?

A: Yes, autism can be genetic. It can run in families. It has a strong genetic basis. Many different small variations in genetic codes can contribute to having autism. The genes that control brain development are associated with autism spectrum disorders.

Autism is a continuous trait. It varies from very severe and non-verbal in some people to social awkwardness in brilliant individuals.

Q: Can a child be gifted and still have autism?

A: There are many kids with autism who are gifted in one area of learning, and may have a deficit in another. A common pattern is a child who should be in a gifted math class but needs special education for reading. As a child, I was good at art and reading. Follow your good instincts when working with these kids. You know more than you think you know. Never hold a child back in the area in which he is gifted. That causes frustration.

Q: What would happen if everyone had autism?

A: The world would be much more logical if everyone had a little autism.

My History and Experiences

Among the most common questions people ask me relate to my own personal life experiences, and how I got to the place I am now. People want to know about my successes, struggles, and general life experiences. I am happy to share my answers here.

Q: What did your mother do right when raising you?

A: My mother was always gently encouraging me to do new things. She knew how to "stretch" me to learn many skills. There should NEVER be sudden surprises. It is a mistake to overprotect a child with autism. I have seen too many children whose parents do all the talking for them. Many of these kids have not learned to shake hands. When I was seven and eight, I learned social skills by being a hostess at my mother's parties.

Q: How did you deal with teasing in high school?

A: When I was teased in high school, my only refuge was friends with shared interests. The students who were interested in horseback riding and electronics did not tease me. Get children involved with shared activities such as art, music, computer programming, and other activities.

Q: How do you think creativity plays into autism and your life?

A: Creativity means a lot to me. Creativity is the process of thinking up new ideas. My mind is highly associative. For example, if I think about soccer balls, my mind starts going through the pictures of balls I have stored in memory. In my imagination, I see baseballs that were on display in a sports restaurant and the ball that drops on New Year's Eve in Times Square. Help a child with autism to broaden his or her art skill and to draw or paint many different things. If the child draws the same cartoon character over and over, suggest he or she draws the character's house or car.

Q: I am fascinated by your brain scans. Can I go to the hospital, get an MRI, and see the layout of my brain's functioning?

A: A plain basic MRI does not show the white fiber tracts that really give insights into the function of the brain circuits. This technology is not out in the hospitals yet. The experimental brain scan studies I have done have confirmed that my deficits and abilities have a basis in the brain. I recommend you work on developing your areas of strength.

(Additional resource: *Thinking in Pictures*)

Q: Where do you find the courage and self-esteem to put your whole life out there? I wish I could be able not to worry about what people think and not be shy and hide away. How do you do it? What's going on in your mind when you're confronted with some kind of social gathering?

A: The first talk I gave in grad school, I panicked and walked out. Overcoming your fears is a gradual process. In learning not to be afraid, you just have to get out there and do it!

Q: How did you deal with temper tantrums growing up? How did your parents react?

A: When I had a temper tantrum, there was always a consequence. After I had calmed down, mother would calmly tell me there would be no TV tonight. She took away TV for only one night. After I calmed down, she always informed me she was enforcing the consequences. The rules were clear. I knew a temper tantrum would always result in one night with no TV. In high school, I got into several fist fights. The consequence was no horseback riding for two weeks. Somehow, I switched from anger to crying. Instead of getting angry when kids teased me, I cried. Changing anger to crying enabled me to have a career. Crying at a meat plant is not socially acceptable and I hid in the basement or the cattle pens and did it in private. Hitting people would have resulted in no career.

Q: In *Emergence: Labeled Autistic,* you said you are a recovered autistic, but now you seem to embrace your autism. What happened?

A: I wrote *Emergence* in 1986. Today, I would never use the term "recovered autistic." I have learned how to adapt to my condition and improve. Brain scans done on me as an adult indicate I am still autistic. Help your son to develop his strengths.

(Additional resource: *The Way I See It*)

Q: Does looking at other peoples' faces and their different expressions bother you at all?

A: Other people's facial expressions do not bother me. I just never understood the really subtle changes in expression.

Q: My baby is three years old and has autism, and I want her to be happy. Were you happy as a kid, a teenager? Are you happy now?

A: Yes, I was very happy as a kid. However, during my teen years, I had lots of teasing.

It is very important that your child gets early intervention therapy as soon as possible.

If you look on my website, www.templegrandin.com, you will see one of my frequently asked questions, Question 1, talks about the importance of early intervention and therapy for a young child. It is possible to begin therapies as young as 18 months. Join a local support group and find resources in your area.

Q: Do you feel your ability to visualize the world and your ideas has improved with each achievement in your life?

A: Thank you for your email regarding my visualization.

Visualization gets better as I have more and more experiences. With each experience come images I can use for my visual library.

This is why it is important to get kids out and have them experience many different and interesting things.

Q: I am sorry this is not an actual question. However, Temple, I am a special education teacher in Australia working with many autistic children, and have just watched your movie (HBO). I have to say that my eldest child and I sat there totally enthralled at your story (he has many traits of ASD, but falls in the gray area of the spectrum). I commend you on your life works and allowing your story to be told in such an effective way. You have certainly opened my eyes to the inner mind of someone who has autism in a way I have never been able to see through my young students, who often are not able to convey this. So, I would like to say thank you; you are indeed an inspiration to me and I will be using you as an example to some of my students when they feel it is all just too hard. Life is just opening another door for them, and you have for me.

A: Thank you for your email and your kind words. It makes me happy to be seen as a leader for young people.

I am happy that you liked the HBO movie. I think Claire Danes did a great job of portraying me.

I am glad you think the movie is inspirational.

Life Skills

Another big topic is about general life skills people with autism and sensory issues may battle with. As always, I am willing to share whatever advice might be helpful.

Q: Do you have any suggestions for teaching ASD kids to drive?

A: Kids on the spectrum can learn to drive, but they need lots and lots of practice! Practice in learning the basic operation of a car; steering, braking, backing up, acceleration, etc.

When I learned to drive, I had one year on easy, back-country roads before I drove in traffic and on freeways. The best place to start is a large deserted parking lot. Let them practice turning, parking, backing up, stopping, acceleration, etc.

If a child has ridden a bike safely and followed the rules, he or she can learn to drive.

(Additional resource: *The Way I See It,* page 297: "Can my adolescent drive a car?"

Q: My husband gets seasonal affective disorder, and tends to become very depressed in winter. Any advice for him?

A: I get depressed in November and December, and light therapy helps me. I get up at 6 am and sit next to a full-spectrum LED light for 30 minutes. The principle is to extend my photoperiod so it is like summer. You can look up scientific papers for light therapy on Google Scholar.

Q: Dear Temple, I have been working with my only son for 28 years. He has Asperger's and has just graduated from university with a commercial music major. He is waiting to go to graduate school in Canada. He felt he can do better in recording arts and technologies. It will be a one-year master's degree program. Our concern is his ability to live alone and handle the legal issues after he outlives me and my husband. As you can see, he is smart at his studies and probably will get a job in the area he chooses. But we are worried how he is going to deal with the real world and many tricky people. To us, he is very kind and only can view society positively. Please share your thoughts with me on this issue and please also suggest if we need to create a trust fund for someone to take care of the assets, investment, and money issues. Thank you for your help in advance!

A: Thank you for your email regarding your son.

For someone who has never lived away from home, it may be best to make a slow transition for him to independent living. Maybe he could get an apartment locally, close by, before moving to Canada. That way, family and friends would be close should he need any help, and they could check in on him.

As for the trust fund, you would need to seek legal counsel—that is out of my area of expertise

Q: Temple, I have a 19-year-old son with Asperger's, and I have a question. How do I get him to stick to a schedule? He lives alone and is getting lost as to how to keep a schedule.

A: It helps me to have a calendar to use for my scheduling. The one I have is an entire month at a glance—all on one sheet of paper.

Seeing the entire month really helps me to see everything written out for the month so I know what to expect.

You may try posting copies of the month's calendar on his wall and on his refrigerator and then suggesting he keep a copy on his person at all times.

Q: My son doesn't like playing games, because he always wants it to be his turn. Should I just not try to play games with him?

A: It is extremely important to teach turn taking. Board games are an excellent way to teach young children turn taking. Kids have to learn how to wait for their turn.

Q: My son has autism and was very close to his grandfather, who has just passed away. How do I explain death to him?

A: It is better to give a simple concrete answer. If your nephew has ever seen an animal die, you can tell him that when people and animals get old, they die and do not come back. Never tell him that grandpa fell asleep and died or went on a trip. That will cause fear of trips or going to sleep.

Q: Dr. Grandin, before I ask you my question(s) I would first like to thank you for your insight into autism! You helped me to recognize that I can see autism as a gift rather than a downfall, and that is an invaluable gift you have given me! My first question concerns my five-year-old high-functioning boy with autism. He is VERY argumentative. He sees things a certain way and there is NO talking him out of it. He just does not grasp that we (the parents) are in charge, and that he is a child, and unfortunately, yes, he does have to listen to us. Do you know how we can deal with him in a way he will grasp? Thank you so much, Dr. Grandin!

A: The main thing is to be consistent and constant with the consequences. If your son is defiant, then no television, no video games, etc. for the evening. Another way to avoid defiant behavior is to stop using the word 'no.' When the child makes a mistake, give an instruction instead of saying no. For example, if the child eats mashed potatoes with his hands, say, "use the fork." You should also provide advice such as, "You can do your homework after school or after dinner."

It is also equally important that good behavior is rewarded.

In every conversation with him, be very calm and matter of fact with your speech. Never threaten to take something away during a tantrum or a meltdown. Wait until the child calms down.

Q: Hello, Temple! I am curious how people with autism develop loving relationships with family members, friends, and animals. You mentioned you have little interest in reading or talking about relationships, and I understand that people with autism have little interest and much difficulty relating to others in social environments. I know every person with autism is different, but overall, do most people with autism experience emotions (i.e., love) differently than people without autism? Does the lack of social interest affect the way they emotionally bond with others? Thank you for your consideration and taking the time to read my question. I consider myself to be a lifelong learner and I am eager to learn more from you.

A: I find that I basically build bonds with people through shared interests. In high school, it was horseback riding and electronics lab. Now, as an adult, I have formed friendships with individuals in the animal welfare and meat industry.

I do have emotions and they are very strong. However, they are simple, and not complex. I can be happy, sad, or angry. Emotions are like an afternoon thunderstorm, and I never hold grudges.

I have replaced emotional complexities with intellectual complexities.

(Additional resource: *Thinking in Pictures*)

Q: How should I prepare my child for a trip to the mall? He often gets overwhelmed there.

A: Children with autism panic when there are surprises. To help a child tolerate a mall or an airport he/she needs to know a lot about it BEFORE they go. Show the child lots of videos and pictures and explain procedures such as security. He/she should visit the TSA website so security procedures are not a surprise. Make the mall as familiar as possible. Do this BEFORE you go. For the first few trips, go when the mall is quiet and has fewer people.

(Additional resource: *The Way I See It*)

Q: How can I get my teenage son with autism to be more social?

A: Find something he is good at, such as art, sports, music, or scouting, he can enjoy with others. He needs to start learning some work skills such as walking dogs for the neighbors or working in a farmer's market. Get him out doing things. He should NOT be sitting at home playing video games.

Q: My son loves to play video games. He would rather do this than go outside and play. How do I get him to play with kids instead of the video?

A: You need to gradually wean him away. Video games have the same effect as stimming. Try gradually reducing the time he plays games. Reward him for doing other activities. He may be better at socializing with adults. Find activities he enjoys that he can do with other people, such as scouting, building robots, or playing in a band. Try taking turns playing a video game with a single controller that must be shared.

Non-Verbal

One of the more challenging aspects of autism is presented when the child is non-verbal. Parents and teachers always want to know how best to reach a child who does not easily communicate back.

Q: My daughter is non-verbal and has recently started throwing tantrums. What can I do to help her, and me?

A: A major cause of tantrums in a non-verbal child is sensory overload. If the tantrum occurs in a noisy place, sensory overload is probably the reason. You also need to check for hidden painful medical problems like acid reflux, toothaches, constipation, or ear infections. These may be the cause of the child's problems.

(Additional resource: *The Way I See It*)

Q: I have a student who is non-verbal, with severe sensory issues. Most of the time she is anxious and irritable to the point of throwing tantrums, but sometimes when there are loud sounds, she actually calms down. Are the loud noises good for her?

A: Sometimes when a child with sensory problems is very calm, he or she is in a state of sensory shutdown. You also must rule out painful hidden medical problems that your child may not be telling you about. Some of the most common problems are acid reflux (heartburn), yeast infections, and earaches.

(Additional resource: *The Way I See It* and *The Autistic Brain*)

Q: How do I best communicate with my non-verbal child?

A: Some non-verbal children with autism do well with sign language. To develop really complex speech, typing is often better. A tablet computer is recommended because the type appears next to the keyboard. On a laptop or desktop, the child has to look up to see the print, and is not able to make the attention shift.

Q: My three-year-old grandson has been diagnosed as autistic. He will be four in September and still does not speak. I am desperate for information on how I can help him. I cannot seem to get through to him; eye contact is still not very good. He also has a slight deletion on chromosome 16. Do you have any insight into this condition?

A: Thank you for your question regarding your three-year-old grandson. Due to the fact that he remains non-verbal, you must get him into an early intervention program now! Such as program will give him the therapies he needs. I cannot express strongly enough the importance of doing this as soon as possible.

You may also want to Google and join a support group in your City/State where you can meet other family members and parents who could suggest good clinics and a therapist for your grandson. Please see the next question, as well, for more information.

Q: How do I teach my young non-verbal child?

A: The most important thing you can do with a child under five years old, who has no language or developmental delays, is to organize many hours a week of one-on-one teaching with an effective teacher. Research shows that 20 to 30 hours per week of one-on-one teaching is most effective. If your financial resources are limited, get some volunteer grandmothers or students to help. Teach words and do lots of turn-taking games. Don't wait – doing nothing is the WORST thing you can do.

(Additional resource: *The Way I See It*)

Education and Learning

Another big topic is the education and learning experiences of children (and adults) with autism and sensory issues. It is imperative for each child to be educated as much as possible. On the following pages you will find some of my advice on learning and current learning technologies.

Q: Can a child learn language by watching television?

A: Watching TV is a bad idea. My speech teacher taught me to speak by gently encouraging me to get my words out. To build up the circuits requires ACTIVE participation and not passive participation like watching TV. All children learn best when they interact with real people.

Q: How do you feel about children's books as apps? Are these better for learning?

A: Research shows children's books should be free of all links and videos. The best books parents can read to their young children are either paper or eBooks that show just text and pictures with no links, audio, or videos to distract the child's attention.

Q: My son is three and we have been trying ABA treatment with him, but I am not sure it is working. Should we stop?

A: I would recommend continuing to do ABA, which is an evidence-based treatment. He needs to have about 20 hours a week of ABA-type instruction with an effective teacher. If there is a cost issue, get some volunteers who can be coached by the ABA teacher. I did not talk until I was four. You may also want to have an OT do some sensory activities with him. Your child needs to be kept engaged with the world. Watching TV and computer time should be limited to one hour a day.

(Additional resource: *The Way I See It*)

Q: What do you think about kids with autism using an iPad as a learning tool?

A: Make interfaces really simple. It is also best to avoid a lot of colored backgrounds and colored lettering. Keep it simple. People on the spectrum love iPads and other tablets with user-friendly icons. Many people on the spectrum like typing on an iPad because they can look at both the virtual keyboard and the print they are typing at the same time. An iPad or any other electronic device should never be used to replace interaction with real people.

Q: I've heard a lot about hippotherapy. Do you recommend using horses to teach kids with autism or sensory issues?

A: There is a huge need to document how some individuals respond in such a positive way to horses. Some children say their first words on a horse. Autism is very variable—some individuals respond well to equine therapy and others do not. There are some scientific studies. You can look them up in Google Scholar or the PubMed databases. These databases are free, and summaries of research articles are free. Type *PubMed* or *Google Scholar* into Google to access these scientific databases.

Q: My daughter is six and is autistic. She loves animals, books, and music. My question is, how did you find your way of life? Was it through certain passions, and how do I encourage my daughter through her passions.

A: I am assuming your daughter has a passion for dogs. If that is so, then teach her with dogs. Teach math with dogs, by calculating how fast they run, teach history with dogs, by looking up the history of animals, teach her reading with dogs, etc. If it is appropriate, then let her have a pet and let her accept sole responsibility for its care.

Q: What is the most important design feature for a school for kids with autism?

A: The most important design feature for a school for autistic children is to have no florescent lights. Some children with autism can see the 50-cycle flicker of florescent lights. It makes the room look like a flashing strobe light. Highly contrasting patterns such as stripes or checkerboards should be avoided.

Q: I heard you mention some free learning websites that are good for kids with autism. What were those again?

A: The free learning websites are:

Khan Academy – www.khanacademy.org

Udacity – www.udacity.com

Stanford Free Classes – http://online.stanford.edu/courses

Wolfram Mathematica – www.wolfram.com/mathematica

Codecademy – www.codecademy.com

Makezine.com – http://makezine.com *(not free, but has fun stuff)*

Q: Do you recommend music therapy for young non-verbal children?

A: Some children with autism can learn to sing words before they can speak them. Singing and talking use different brain currents. Music therapy can be helpful for some children with autism.

Q: My son reads a lot, but never seems to "get it." How do I help him with reading comprehension?

A: Children may be able to decode words easily, but their comprehension may be poor. I would recommend using Reading 1 materials about very clear, concrete subjects. Pick things the child can visualize when he/she reads. When you test for comprehension, ask concrete questions. Use books that cover subjects the children are interested in. If the book is about football, ask concrete questions such as which team won the game or what was the color of the winning team's uniforms?

Q: How did you learn to tell time?

A: I learned to tell the time on a big clock which had a minute hand I could see move. Every minute I could see it move slightly. Then I understood the passage of time. The clock was a large classroom clock.

Q: My daughter cannot seem to understand colors. What do we do?

A: Teaching colors as an abstract concept will not work. Color will have to have meaning. She may learn better if colors are linked to something she cares about, such as food. She may be able to learn that her favorite food is in the blue containers, or that carrots are orange.

Q: Hello, I have an 11-year-old daughter, who was diagnosed with autism at the age of six. She is very verbal (sometimes too much so) and may lean more towards Asperger's in some ways. She does have challenges with learning, reading comprehension, fine/gross motor skills (e.g., tying her shoelaces, etc.), and socializing (making and maintaining friendships). How can we help her understand things or improve reading comprehension?

A: Start by answering very concrete questions about a story. For example in a story about going to the North Pole, you might ask: *How many people were on the team? What color was Jim's coat? What breed of dog pulled the sled?*

Don't ask: *Why are winter coats needed at the North Pole?* To answer this question, the child would have to have general knowledge about the North Pole; for instance, it is very cold at the North Pole. If you did not know that, you could not answer the question.

To fully answer questions about a story or article on the North Pole, you would have to have enough knowledge about the North Pole to answer them.

You must have basic knowledge about the subject in order to answer questions about it.

Similarly, if you read a story about touchdowns, you would have to know about football in order to answer questions about touchdowns.

Q: Dr. Grandin, if you could give only one piece of advice to teachers and one piece of advice to parents, what would they be?

A: The advice I would give to teachers and/or parents would be to develop the child's strengths and teach them from those. For instance, if a child likes art, then teach with art, if they like trains, then teach with trains, dinosaurs, etc. You can teach math with trains, you can teach art with trains, and so forth.

It also helps the child to develop their interest further by broadening it out. They can learn history by studying parts of the world where dinosaurs once lived.

An interesting fact is that dinosaurs once lived at Denver Airport!

Q: Dear Dr. Grandin, I am a transportation supervisor for a large public school system. I teach and train over 450 special needs drivers and bus monitors. For the past few years the greatest challenge I've encountered is teaching drivers and monitors how to relate to children with autism, specifically Asperger's, so we are able to transport them safely. I have shared information about you in many of my safety meetings, encouraging them to learn about autism so they will be more receptive to children who are more challenging. After 35 years in transportation working with special needs children I am still trying to make a difference for them. Can you suggest any DVDs or materials that would benefit school bus drivers and their monitors regarding autism?

A: Thank you for your question about bus drivers and monitors.

I think it would be beneficial for your drivers and monitors to realize change is the biggest problem for children affected by autism. Any sudden change in routine, a new bus, or a new driver or worker, needs to be told to the children to prepare them for what is to come. If possible, show them a photo of the new bus, the new driver, worker, etc. before the change arrives. No surprises! Secondly, loud noises irritate them. It is important to remember that.

(Additional resources: *The Way I See It* and *Thinking in Pictures*)

Q: What should teachers keep in mind when teaching kids with autism?

A: I think the most important thing for classroom teachers to keep in mind is the sensory issues these children face. A big one is florescent lighting, which can cause real problems for a child in the classroom. Another sensory issue is the noise levels in the cafeteria and the gym.

Q: Hi, Dr. Grandin, I am currently enrolled in a doctoral program and am presently taking a course in assistive technology. For this class, we are reading your books. I am reading "Thinking in Pictures," which I selected because I spent 20 years as a high school art teacher 1 and witnessed first-hand how my students with Asperger's were my most creative and detail-oriented students. I have also viewed your TED video and cheered when you spoke about how we need these students! I am wondering if you could tell what you believe are the most important things we as classroom teachers and school administrators need to know/do to meet the needs of students with autism? I have worked in schools designed to meet the needs of students with autism spectrum disorders and found that once they were sent back to their regular schools, they often met with failure. What do we as educators need to learn to provide our autistic students with opportunities to succeed in school? Thank you so much for your time, Dr. Grandin.

A: 1. They need to understand sensory problems. Have them read the sensory chapter in my book *The Autistic Brain*. Sometimes accommodations have to be made for sensory oversensitivity.

2. Slow down when talking and enunciate words—written instructions are sometimes better because remembering long strings of verbal information is difficult.

3. Build and develop special strengths a child may have in art, math, or reading. Emphasize strengths.

4. Teach social skills such as shaking hands and saying *please* and *thank you*.

5. Get the child involved in activities in which there are shared interests with other children such as art, music, math, or making cool stuff.

    (Additional resource: *The Autistic Brain*)

Squeeze Machine

One thing people are still fascinated by is my squeeze machine, which I developed while in college to ease my anxieties. I am happy that this same machine has helped countless other people with autism and sensory issues.

Q: Where can you buy a body-pressing machine and how much do they cost? Are they safe for kids about age eight?

A: You can Google "squeeze machine" or "big hug" and find the building plans for my squeeze machine. I must warn you though, it is not a project for beginners.

Some alternatives to the squeeze machine would be to roll the child up in gym mats to achieve the proper amount of pressure. You can also let them lay under sofa cushions. Sometimes weighted vests or blankets work, too.

Q: Do you still use the Hug Machine? Do you know if other autistic people get comfort from this? You are amazing.

A: My squeeze machine broke in 2010 and I have been too busy to fix it. I do not need it as much now, as I am getting more hugs from real people.

Many autistic people get comfort from a hug, or the squeeze that comes from a hug. There are other things to try besides a machine; weighted blankets or vests, rolling up in gym mats or under the couch cushions for pressure.

I have a published paper on the Hug Machine. The article is: "Calming effects of deep touch pressure in patients with autistic disorders, college students, and animals," *Journal of Child and Adolescent Psychiatry*, Vol. 2, pp. 63-70 (Grandin, T. 1992).

Q: My son is seven. He is autistic and non-verbal, with very high energy! He seems to find comfort in being hugged or hugging his blankets. It has been suggested he might benefit from a restrictive device, such as a blanket with Velcro straps we could tighten to give him constrictive pressure. We would use it when he gets very agitated and is looking for deep-pressure stimulation. When I heard this suggestion, I thought about the device you talk about using (not sure what you call it). I think he is looking for a way to channel his energy, but he gets so agitated that he jumps from one thing to the next without ever really grasping the task or lesson at hand.

A: Many autistic people like the sense of a "hug." The suggestion of a blanket with Velcro straps is a good one, but you may want to try rolling him up in gym mats for the pressure he needs. Another idea would be to let him lay under sofa cushions, with you applying small amounts of pressure.

Weighted vests and blankets work well, too.

Q: Hi, Temple. I am 10, and I really LOVED your movie! It is my favorite movie ever! I loved your project that had to do with optical illusions! I would never have figured that out if I hadn't watched your movie. I was wondering are you still friends with your blind roommate from college? Have you ever made a squeeze machine for anyone else? Lastly, at your aunt's ranch, do you still have your handiwork at the gate up?

A: I am glad you liked the HBO movie. Yes, I am still friends with my roommate from college. We lost contact for many years, but after the HBO movie came out, she contacted me.

I have made a squeeze machine for the Therafin Corporation. They sell it commercially on their website. You can also Google "Hug Machine" and see the drawings on the Internet.

As for the gate at my aunt's ranch, unfortunately, the ranch was sold a long time ago and the gate is no longer in service. Thank you for your questions. Study hard and do well in school.

Annotated Important Further Reading

Grandin, T. and Panek, R. (2013) *The Autistic Brain, Helping Different Kinds of Minds to Succeed*, Houghton Mifflin, NY

> Contains easy-to-read summaries of research studies on sensory oversensitivity, and reviews literature on different kinds of thinking.

Grandin, T. (1995) *Thinking in Pictures*, Vintage (Random House), New York

> Original description of my visual thinking and my personal experiences with anxiety and panic attacks. I describe how low-dose antidepressants stopped my anxiety.

Green, S. A. et al. (2013) Overreactive brain responses to sensory stimuli in youth with autism spectrum disorders, *Journal of the America Academy of Child and Adolescent Psychiatry*, 52:1158-1172.

> Study done with a functional MRI that shows the autistic brain overreacts to intense sound or visual stimuli. Intense sensory stimuli also activate emotional centers such as the amygdala in people with autism. This may explain why intense sensory stimulation causes fear.

Kozhevnikov, M., et al. (2005). Spatial versus object visualizers: A new characterization of visual cognitive style, *Memory and Cognition*, 33:710-726.

An early paper where Maria Kozhevnikov first presents evidence of two types of visual thinkers. They are the object visualizer, like me, and the spatial pattern mathematic thinker.

Kozhevnikov, M. (2013) Creativity, visualization abilities and visual cognitive style, *British Journal of Educational Psychology*, 83:196-209.

Extensive visual spatial, object visual, and verbal creativity tests administered show that objective visualizers, spatial visualizers, and verbally creative people are distinct thinking types.

Mazard, A., et al. (2004) A PET meta-analysis of object and spatial mental imagery, *European Journal of Cognitive Psychology*, 16:673-695.

PET brain scan study of individuals performing difficult mental rotation tasks (spatial imagery) and object imagery tasks such as visualizing landmarks in a park or making pictures, such as a lion, from words. The brain scan clearly indicated that the two types of visual thinking activated different parts of the brain.

Woo, C.C. and Leon, M. (2013) Environmental Enrichment is an Effective Treatment for Autism: A Randomized Controlled Trial, *Behavioral Neuroscience*.

This paper describes an innovative study that found continually changing sensory stimulation of two different senses brought about improvements in children with autism. The method is based on three principles:

1. Stimulate two senses simultaneously
2. One of the senses is always smell, touch, or balance
3. Novelty, and changing the stimulation

r. Grandin's insights into animal behavior and her innovations in livestock handling have revolutionized food-animal welfare. Along the way, Grandin has also inspired people around the world as a champion for individuals with autism and their families.

Her accomplishments as a speaker, author and advocate earned her a place among *Time* magazine's "100 Most Influential People" in 2010, and her life story was the subject of the acclaimed 2010 HBO biopic, *Temple Grandin*, winner of seven Emmy awards and a Golden Globe.

Temple is world-famous for using insights gained from her autism to lead dramatic improvements in the livestock industry. A professor at Colorado State University for more than 20 years, she is a celebrated speaker who lectures internationally on autism and livestock handling.

TEMPLE DID IT, AND I CAN, TOO!

A Child's Guide to Reaching Life Goals

$14.95 | HARDCOVER | COMING SEPTEMBER 2015!

CPSIA information can be obtained at www.ICGtesting.com
Printed in the USA
BVOW08s0255240315

392837BV00006B/4/P